TOPICS IN MEDIEVAL HISTORY
Edited by DAVID J. HALL

Towns and Traders/GILLIAN DAY

WITH DRAWINGS BY ROY SCHOFIELD

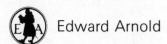 Edward Arnold

© Gillian Day 1974
First published 1974
by Edward Arnold (Publishers) Ltd.,
41 Bedford Square, London WC1B 3DQ

Reprinted 1979

ISBN: 0 7131 1830 X

The series comprises:
Crafts and Craftsmen by Christopher Chappell
Villages and Farming by Marilyn Chappell
People and Places by Gillian Day
Towns and Traders by Gillian Day
Knights and Castles by David J. Hall
Monks and Monastries by David J. Hall

Set in 10 on 12 pt. Univers light by Keyspools Limited, Golborne
and printed in Great Britain by Butler & Tanner Ltd., Frome

Contents

Acknowledgments

The Publishers' thanks are due to the following for permission to use photographs reproduced in this book:

British Museum (pp. 6, 14, 15 *left*, 40);
Chester City Record Office (p. 7 *top*);
Aerofilms Ltd (pp. 7 *bottom*, 16 *top*);
Bibliothèque Nationale, Paris (pp. 10, 13, 37 *bottom*);
Radio Times Hulton Picture Library (pp. 15 *right*, 21, 24, 25, 27, 29 *right*, 31, 32, 37 *top*, 47 *top and bottom left*);
Royal Commission on Historical Monuments — Crown Copyright (p. 16 *bottom*);
Public Record Office (p. 19 *top*);
National Monuments Record (p. 19 *bottom*);
Guildhall Art Gallery (p. 20);
Camera Press Ltd (p. 23);
The Company of the Merchant Adventurers of the City of York (p. 28);
York City Council (pp. 33, 34, 35, 47 *top left*);
The Wellcome Institute of the History of Medicine — by courtesy of the Trustees (pp. 38, 43);
Mansell Collection (pp. 41 *bottom*, 44 *top left and right*);
Trinity College, Cambridge (pp. 39, 41 *top*);
British Tourist Authority (pp. 44 *bottom*, 45);

Thanks are also due to the author and publisher of *Brasses and Brass Rubbing* by Clare Gittings (Blandford Press) for permission to use the photograph reproduced on p. 22, and to James Osborne for permission to use the drawing of the Woolpack Inn on p. 25.

To the Reader

This book describes Towns and Traders from the Norman Conquest to A.D. 1500 — the Middle Ages or medieval times as it is often called.

The information is given in the written part of each chapter and in the photographs, drawings and descriptions of the pictures. At the end of each section there are questions for you to answer in your note books. You will also find it helpful to copy some of the drawings into your books.

You should compare present day towns and people with those described in the book. List all the differences and try to find out why they have changed. Your teacher will help you to do this.

1 Sites of Medieval Towns

Most medieval towns were no bigger than a present day village. They were enclosed by a stone wall or by a wooden fence on top of an earth bank. Inside the town, you would have seen many small, thatched wooden houses in streets so narrow that the tops of the buildings nearly touched each other. It was very noisy and animals wandered freely past the houses, or stopped to root in the heaps of rubbish which littered the streets. The largest buildings were the churches and the houses of rich merchants. Only the rich houses had gardens because land was expensive.

Why did people live in towns?

One reason was safety. The walls which you can see in the picture of a medieval town gave protection from enemy attack. Other towns grew up near the stone castles built by the Normans. Rochester in Kent is a good example of this type. Trade was another reason why towns grew in importance. As pedlars travelled round England buying or selling goods, the villages, where they stayed and paid for food and shelter, grew richer. Neighbouring villagers who heard about this came to live there too.

Some examples of places where medieval towns developed:

1   Dover had a castle and a good harbour so people moved there to trade with merchants from abroad. You can see a picture of Dover castle opposite.
2   A town grew in Cambridge near a bridge over the river, and at Winchester where six roads met.
3   The abbey of St Albans needed extra workers to help the monks. These workers built houses near the abbey and so the town of St Albans developed.
4   The Romans had built a town at

Chester and in the plan on this page you can see how the builders of medieval Chester kept the straight lines of Roman town roads. They also used a bend in the River Dee to give extra protection to their town.

5 In Bath, houses were built round the hot water springs, which from Roman times to the present day, were used to help people with rheumatism.

Medieval towns were often given nicknames: Proud Preston, Drunken Bidford, Canny Newcastle, Hungry Grafton, and they had their local heroes: Nottingham and Robin Hood, Coventry and Peeping Tom.

Things to do

1 *Complete these sentences using the words in the box.*
Medieval towns were the size of a present day ....
They were enclosed by a stone .... or a wooden ....
A town grew in Dover because it had a good ...., and ....
The Romans had built a town at ....

> fence, village, harbour, Chester, wall, castle

2 *Draw or trace the plan of medieval Chester.*

3 *Make a list of some of the differences between a medieval town and a modern town.*

4 *Can you say why towns grew up in Cambridge, Winchester, St Albans and Bath?*

2 A rich merchant.

CESTRIA VVLGO CHESTER ANGLIÆ *Civitas*

3 Plan of medieval Chester.
4 Dover Castle keep.

2 Streets

1   A town street.

Town houses were built close together in terraces and the tall houses kept the narrow streets almost always in shadow. The surface of the street was sometimes made of large stones called cobbles, but usually it was just beaten earth which became muddy when it rained. There were few pavements and townsmen had to walk carefully to miss the huge mounds of rotting rubbish tipped by shopkeepers and householders in the middle of the street. After dark it was easy to fall over this rubbish, for apart from one or two lanterns, there were no street lights. It was safer to walk in the shelter of the houses, to avoid dirty water tipped from an upper floor window into the street. There was no proper rubbish collection or street cleaning such as we have in modern towns. Instead, when officers called scavengers received a lot of complaints about the flies and smell from the decaying filth, they arranged for it to be carted away from the streets and dumped in a river.

Not many people travelled far from their own town and so the townsman knew most of the people he met in the street. He was suspicious of strangers, especially in Coventry, where the citizens were warned about their rude behaviour and readiness to throw half bricks at visitors. The streets were noisy, particularly when a game of football was in progress. Football was played without rules, referee or fixed goals. It became a fight between rival gangs to kick the ball through the streets from one end of the town to the other, causing broken arms and legs and terrifying people who were in their way. On quieter days, the towns-people walked to the market place in the middle of the town to listen to the town-crier calling out the news.

Transport was by horse or horse drawn cart. Funeral carts, horses pulling heavy farm carts, heavily-laden pack horses and people on horseback clattered down the street. Since the horse was the most important means of transport there were different types for different jobs. There were ambling nags for priests and ladies, and huge sturdy farm horses. A rich young man rode a fast fiery charger with brightly coloured bridle and reins, and this was the shiny, polished equivalent of a modern sportscar.

2 Cart.

3 Packhorse.

4 Footballer.

5 Town-crier.

Things to do

1 *Complete these sentences using the words in the box.*
Officials called .... organised the collection of rubbish and dumped it in a river.
The .... called out the daily news.
The .... was the most important method of transport.

town-crier, scavengers, horse

2 *Why did the streets smell?*
3 *Find out where the authorities in your town dump household rubbish.*
4 *How does the modern game of Association Football differ from the medieval game?*

9

3 Shops

1   Shops.

In most towns shops selling the same type of goods were found together in one street. In London corn was sold on Cornhill, candles in Candlemakers' Row, meat in Butchers' Row and tailors worked in Threadneedle Street.

Modern supermarkets have departments selling food, furniture and clothes, which shoppers can see through large glass windows. A medieval shop in a small ground-floor room sold only one kind of article. Wooden shutters covered the open window space of the shop front and could be let down to form a counter. Behind the counter was the workroom with a table, shelves and hooks for the food to stand or hang upon. Customers could watch the shopkeeper making the things he sold. Painted picture signs outside the shops showed what they sold—this was necessary because few people could read. The shopkeeper lived in a room behind the shop.

Shops in some towns were famous for special kinds of food, for instance Barnstaple ginger-bread, Coventry god-cakes and Banbury cheese. The taverns in each town were easy to find with their bushes of fresh green leaves hanging outside. Each tavern brewed its own ale, unlike today when beer is made in factories and delivered to the public houses in large tankers. Brewers were usually women. After every brew was made, the tavern hung out its "ale stake", which was a long pole with a bunch of fresh green leaves at the end. Town officials called ale-tasters

drank some of the new ale and if it tasted nasty the tavern might have to close. If the tasters liked it, the publican could sell the ale for one silver penny a gallon.

This was the only coin used in shops in England until the end of the thirteenth century for there was no paper money. Shopkeepers were not allowed to charge high prices and make a big profit for themselves. In Chester, where the butchers went on strike because they were not allowed to charge higher prices for their meat, the mayor had them put into prison.

Some brewers and butchers were punished for selling bad food and drink. The brewer had to drink some of her bad ale and have the rest poured over her head. The dishonest butcher had to stand in the pillory while his rotten meat was burnt in front of him.

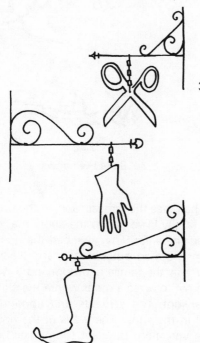

3   Shop signs.

Things to do

1   Draw or trace the picture of the shops. Can you label the barber's shop and the shops which sold fur, cloth and groceries?
2   Look at the shop signs drawn on the page near these questions. What did the shops sell?
3   What would you buy in a shop with an ale-stake sign outside?

4 Houses

1   House and stables.

2   Barred windows.

In towns the rich merchants built their houses close together with rooms on two or three floors. This was because land was expensive within the town walls. The shop or workroom was on the ground floor facing the street. Behind the shop was a hall, a store room and a kitchen. You can see that part of the storage space in the picture was used as a stable for the horses.

The hall was the largest room in the house. The family lived above the shop in a room called the solar. They reached the upstairs rooms from an outside staircase. Near the solar was the family bedroom and a wardrobe, which was a room where the clothes were kept. The servants and apprentices slept in the shop. The walls of the houses were very thin. Burglars sometimes broke into the houses through the walls. They found that this was easier than squeezing through the narrow barred windows. The windows were small because glass was expensive. When a merchant moved to a new house, he took the windows with him because they were very valuable. Inside the house was dim and gloomy. The rooms were lit by candles in large metal

12

lanterns hanging from the ceilings. Carved wooden pictures or lengths of brightly coloured cloth decorated the walls. Embroidered pictures called tapestries showed stories from the Bible and added colour to the dark room. A log fire in the stone fireplace kept the room warm. There was not very much furniture even in the house of a rich merchant. The wooden table and stools at one end of the hall were heavy and plain. There was a carved wooden chair for the master of the house. The large four poster bed upstairs had a feather mattress and thick curtains hung round the bed to keep out draughts. Such a house seems to us cold and gloomy, yet to the medieval merchant's family it had every comfort they could imagine.

In the narrow town streets it was very easy for fire to spread quickly. The thatched roofs and wooden houses soon caught fire. Often large areas of a town were completely destroyed. Each town kept special hooks and ropes in the town centre to pull down the burning thatch and stop the fire from spreading. Merchants built their new town houses of stone and brick to cut down the risk of fire. As you can see in the picture opposite, some houses had tiled roofs. In London, laws stopped people using thatch on the roofs of houses within the City walls.

Things to do

1 *Complete these sentences using the words in the box.*
   The largest room in the house was the ....
   The family lived above the shop in a room called the ....
   The .... was the room where clothes were kept.
   .... roofs and .... houses easily caught fire.

> solar, wardrobe, thatched, hall, wooden

2 *How did medieval townsmen fight fires in burning houses?*
3 *How does a modern fire brigade fight fires?*

3 Fire!

5 Town Charters

1   The granting of a charter.

once a year. It was a very important occasion when a town received its charter as you can see in the picture. Many lords did not want to hand over so much power to the local people. But, when King Richard I, King John, and the nobles were short of money a great many towns bought charters. King John gave a Charter to Liverpool and the Earl of Derby made Bolton a Borough. The townspeople of Hastings, Dover, Sandwich, Romney and Hythe—called the Cinque (Cinque is French for five) Ports—promised to have ships ready for the king, and in return they paid less tax to him. As the towns grew even larger, the craftsmen left the Guild

2   Seal of Hastings.

As villages grew larger and became towns they were ruled by the king, or a great lord or a local abbot. The Lord of Rochester Castle governed Rochester, which was built near his Castle, and the Abbot of St Albans controlled the town of St Albans close by his rich monastery. In return for the lord's protection, the townsmen had to work on his farms for no pay. They had to pay him taxes and all the fines collected in the law courts. As trade increased and the towns grew richer, the townsmen wanted to look after themselves, spend all their time on their own jobs and not pay taxes to their lord. So they joined together in a union called the Guild Merchant, and asked the lord to sell them a charter. This charter was an agreement which allowed the townspeople to choose a town council and mayor, control the law courts and collect their own taxes. It gave them the right to hold a market each week and a fair

Merchant and formed their own craft guilds, for example the grocers' guild and the tailors' guild.

The leaders of the separate guilds became the town council and elected the mayor. The council paid water carriers to take water in carts and buckets to the shops and houses. They also looked after the repair of the town gates and walls, and the roads and bridges within the walls. In order to pay for this work they collected a tax from traders selling goods in the market. A tax called Murage paid for the upkeep of the gates and walls, and Pavage for the upkeep of the roads and bridges.

4   Gateway to King's Lynn.

3   Seal of Canterbury.

You can see a picture of the gate into the town of King's Lynn.

One of the most famous medieval Lord Mayors of London was Richard Whittington. The Pantomime story describes how he made his fortune as a poor apprentice. He sold his cat to the Sultan of the Barbary Coast whose palace was full of rats. Whether that story is true or not, Dick Whittington became rich and was Lord Mayor of London three times. He was a busy and helpful Mayor who arranged for water taps to be put in the street, and built a new Library at Greyfriars. He built houses for the poor and repaired St Bartholomew's Hospital at Smithfield.

Things to do

1   Complete these sentences using the words in the box.

Many towns were given their charters in the reigns of King .... and King ....
Hastings promised to have .... ready for the king.
The tax to pay for the repair of the .... was called Pavage.
.... was a famous Lord Mayor of London.

> Richard I, ships, streets,
> Richard Whittington, John

2   Imagine you are a townsman trying to convince a friend that your town needs a charter. Make a list of your reasons.

3   Give a description in your own words of the story of Richard Whittington still used in Pantomime today.

15

6 TownWalls

Townsmen built walls to protect their town from enemy attack. You can see in the picture of Conway how the walls protected a town. Some towns had defences of earth mounds and wooden fences called stockades. Other towns had tall, solid stone walls wide enough to have a walkway on the top. The only way into, and out of, the town was through the guarded gateways in the walls. The gates were made of oak with iron bars across the back. You can see how an iron portcullis protected Bootham Bar at York. At the gate travellers had to tell the gate-keeper their business before he allowed them in. London gatekeepers stopped lepers from entering and spreading disease inside the City. The gates were opened at dawn and locked at sunset. The walls not only protected the townspeople from attack but stopped outsiders from entering the town. Those who lived outside had to pay money to enter the town if they wanted to buy and sell in the market. Gatekeepers collected this money as traders passed through the gates on market days. The townsmen of York built their walls to protect themselves from attack from Scot-

16

3 King Charles' Tower, Chester walls.

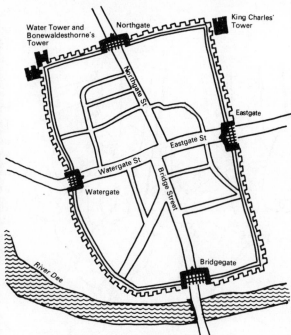
5 Town walls and gates at Chester.

4 Water Tower, Chester walls.

land. Parts of the walls are still there and so are the four great gateways or Bars, called Monk Bar, Walmergate Bar, Micklegate Bar and Bootham Bar. Huge walls protected Chester from Welsh attackers. The top of the wide, red sandstone wall was a walkway for defenders and was reached from inside the town by steep stone staircases. They are still standing and it is possible to walk round the two miles of wall which surrounds the town today as it did in medieval times. On the map you can see the walls and the four main gateways to Chester, Bridgegate, Eastgate, Northgate and Watergate. The Earl of Chester decided who should look after these gates, and provide a gatekeeper to collect the tolls. The Earl of Shrewsbury was responsible for Bridgegate, the Earl of Derby for Watergate, and the Earl of Oxford for Eastgate. The citizens of Chester themselves looked after Northgate. Chester had three interesting towers on the walls. From these towers archers could easily fire arrows at attackers near the base of the wall. The Phoenix Tower on the walls of Chester was rebuilt later and called King Charles' Tower. Here King Charles I watched the Battle of Rowton Moor in the Civil War. The Water Tower helped to guard the northwest angle of the walls. Next to it stood Bonewaldesthorne's Tower built by John de Helpston in 1322. It cost one hundred pounds and has hardly been altered since then.

Things to do

1 Complete these sentences using the words in the box.
   A .... protected Bootham Bar at York.
   Town walls can be seen in................
   Huge walls protected Chester from .... attackers.
   Town gates closed at ....

   sunset, Welsh, York, portcullis

2 Draw or trace the map of the walls of Chester. Fill in the names of four gates. Name the families who looked after these gates.

17

7 Law and Order

1 Sanctuary.

fair. So King Henry II decided that there must be one set of laws, called Common Law, for all the people in England. He chose judges to make certain that they conducted the trials in his courts fairly. Henry divided England into six areas and three judges travelled around each area. The judge called at a town at certain times in the year to hold his court, called an Assize Court. He judged crimes of robbery with violence and murder. Twelve men, who knew something about the crime, gave evidence. So Henry's new laws made certain that the case was decided upon the facts and not upon lies, chance and rumour. Towns which had a

2 Durham Sanctuary knocker.

It was not safe to walk down the narrow streets of the towns at night. A visitor from Europe wrote at the time, "There is no country in the world where there are so many thieves and Robbers as there are in England." A captured robber went before the Baron's Court for trial. People who saw the robbery told their story, but often the barons bribed witnesses to tell untruths or terrorised them with threats of torture. The trials were sometimes also decided by Ordeal. There were three types of Ordeal. In an Ordeal by Fire, the prisoner carried a red hot piece of iron in his hand for three paces. The officers of the baron's court bandaged the prisoner's hand. If, after three days the skin had healed, he was innocent. If the skin remained blistered, he was guilty. For the Ordeal by water, the officers tied up the prisoner with a rope and threw him into a pond. If he floated he was guilty. If he sank he was innocent and, provided he had not drowned, the officers rescued him and set him free. You can see an Ordeal by Combat in the picture opposite. The suspect fought his accuser with special axes and shields and the winner was set free.

These early trials were obviously not

charter held a junior court called a Borough Court. This court tried people for minor crimes but Henry's judges still dealt with the serious ones at the Assize Court. Each town had a small lock-up prison for keeping wrong-doers until they were brought to the borough court. You can see a picture of a prison opposite. If, however, a townsman had damaged the property of the Church, he was not tried in the borough court but was tried and punished in the Church's own court. They did not give the severe punishments handed out by the normal courts. A criminal could make use of the Church to escape capture. For once he got inside a Church, the town's officers could not arrest him. In the picture opposite a criminal is claiming this right called Sanctuary. The picture next to it shows the Durham Cathedral "Sanctuary Knocker". Some people say that criminals escaping from the law held onto it to claim sanctuary. The wrong-doer confessed to his crime at the door of the Church. Then he promised to leave the country and not return, and left the sanctuary bare-headed and barefoot, carrying a wooden cross. He travelled by the most direct route to the coast and took the first ship abroad. Many "Sanctuary Men", however, broke their promises on the journey and settled down in another part of England.

3 Ordeal by combat.

4 A lock-up prison.

Things to do

1   *Complete these sentences using the words in the box.*

A criminal could escape capture inside a church by claiming a right called ....

In Ordeal by fire, if the accused man's hand blistered, he was ....

.... courts punished offences against Church property.

In Ordeal by water, if the suspect sank in the water, the verdict was.............

King Henry II said there must be one law for all people called the .... law.

The .... courts tried serious crimes of robbery with violence and murder.

> sanctuary, common, innocent, assize, Church, guilty

2   *Write a description of Ordeal by fire and Ordeal by water.*
3   *Explain why this method of trial was unfair.*
4   *Make up a story in your own words about a criminal taking sanctuary and then promising to leave the country.*

8 Punishments

Townsfolk had no police force to protect them. Instead the mayor and town officials paid a watchman, called a constable, to arrest thieves and trouble-makers. He was helped by the townspeople themselves who, as soon as he shouted, "Stop thief", came out of their houses to run after the criminal. They called this chase the "hue and cry". When they caught the suspect, they kept him until morning in a dark and often damp prison called a lock-up. You can see a picture of a circular lock-up with a pointed roof. It was built of stone or brick, without windows and it had a heavy iron-barred door. Townsmen called these lock-ups "the clink", a name they borrowed from the famous Clink prison in London. The townsmen had to build and repair the prison. In Chester, the citizens who guarded the Northgate looked after the prison as well. They executed condemned men and punished dishonest shopkeepers. They carried out these duties in return for keeping the toll money they collected on goods which passed through their gate into Chester market. The prisoner went for his trial in the borough court on the morning after his arrest.

These courts dealt with a great many dishonest shopkeepers, and large crowds always came to watch and often to take part in the punishments. Fellow townsmen threw stones, rubbish and rotten vegetables at the guilty traders. They could not escape because their heads and hands were fastened into a wooden board called a pillory. Sometimes the victims' feet were held in the stocks as you can see in the picture. A punishment for bakers who sold underweight loaves is shown below. Horses pulled him through the streets for all to see with the loaf tied round his neck. Richard de Lowes, a London baker, escaped his punishment for selling "brown Bread, not fit for horses to eat". A kind-hearted court set him free because he was an old man and it was winter time. The townsmen had most fun watching the punishments for a complaining, bad-tempered wife. They fastened her into a chair and then ducked her several times in a pond. A wife who scolded and nagged her husband had to wear a scold's bridle which, as you can see in the picture, was a

1   A lock-up.

2   Dishonest baker.

helmet of iron bands. A spiked plate fastened to the bridle fitted into her mouth and stopped her tongue from wagging. Townsmen found guilty of theft in the assize court had much harsher punishments. An ear cut off or an "F" for False burnt on the forehead warned everyone that this man was a thief. For serious robbery and murder the assize court condemned the criminal to death. They were usually hanged but in some coastal towns they were thrown off the cliffs into the sea. In the Isles of Scilly the guilty man was tied to rocks and left to drown at high tide.

3 Stocks.

4 Ducking-stool.

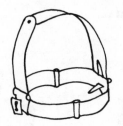

5 Scold's bridle.

Things to do

1 *Complete these sentences using the words in the box.*
A watchman called a .... arrested thieves.
Townspeople threw rotten vegetables to punish dishonest shopkeepers held in the .... and ....
A nagging wife had to wear a .... bridle.
A thief had an .... cut off as his punishment.
In the .... of .... criminals were tied to rocks and left to drown at high tide.

> scold's, ear, stocks, constable, pillory, Isles Scilly

2 *Can you think of any drawbacks to the "hue and cry" method of catching criminals?*
3 *Why did townsmen call their prison "the clink"?*
4 *How did the borough court punish dishonest shopkeepers?*
5 *Draw or trace the picture of the stocks.*

9 The Wool Trade

The Plague called the Black Death killed thousands of farm workers. Afterwards there were too few men to plough the land and sow seed. So the landowners let the grass grow and kept many flocks of sheep, because sheep did not need so many people to look after them. The monasteries owned some of the richest sheep farms. In Kent the Priory of Christchurch at Canterbury kept 1,300 sheep, and in Yorkshire the Cistercian Abbey owned as many. The wool from the English black-faced sheep was the finest in Europe. Weavers turned some of this wool into rough cloth in England, but most of it was sent abroad for making into fine cloth there. The trade with Europe in raw untreated wool, called staple, was England's main source of money. The king took his share of the wealth when he collected a customs duty for each bale of wool sold abroad. In order to make this collection easy, all the wool passed through one town, called the Staple Town. Usually the Staple Town was at Calais in France. Robbers sometimes attacked groups of packhorses carrying wool bales to the ports in England, and pirates robbed the ships at sea during the crossing to Calais. So the wool merchants arranged to travel together in large groups for safety. In Calais they sold the wool to foreign merchants. They made rules for the sale of

1 Wool merchant's feet rest on sheep and woolsack.

2 Woolmark of John Fortey.

3 Wool merchant John Fortey.

22

wool and kept a sharp eye on its quality. A merchant stamped his mark on every bale of wool he sold. The mark showed his initials as you can see in the picture of John Fortey's mark. In spite of the difficult and sometimes dangerous journey to Calais, many wool merchants grew rich and spent their money on building big churches like this one below at Blythburgh in East Anglia.

In England townsmen washed and cleaned the wool which the merchants had not sent abroad. Then they combed it to remove the tangles. They called this process "carding". Women did most of the spinning of wool. The spinner, or spinster, held the wool on a distaff under her arm. The distaff was a wooden stick which held the wool while twisting or spinning it into thread. Finally they wove the thread into cloth. The lady at the back of the picture is

4 Spinning, carding and weaving wool.

5 Blythburgh Church.

weaving on a wooden frame called a loom. Another large sheep farming region besides East Anglia was in the Cotswolds. Northleach was one of the great wool towns there and John Fortey, shown in the picture with a woolsack and sheep beneath his feet, paid for part of Northleach Church.

John Barton, a wool merchant of Holme-beside-Newark, wrote on the stained glass window of his house:

"I thank God and ever shall
It is the sheep hath paid for all."

Things to do

1 *Complete these sentences using the words in the box.*

.... wool was the finest in Europe.

Women called spinsters spun.........
into thread.

Usually the Staple Town was at ....

.... attacked the wool ships.

wool, Calais, English, pirates

10 Thomas Betson

1 Wool Hall at Lavenham.

In the House of Lords there is a large square seat for the Lord Chancellor called a Woolsack. It is covered with fine red cloth and filled with wool. You can see in the pictures of the Wool Hall at Lavenham and the Woolpack Inn at Coggeshall more reminders of the importance of wool in making England wealthy. Thomas Betson spent his life bringing money to England by selling wool to foreign merchants in Calais. He was a Merchant of the Staple who wrote many letters to his wife Katherine. From these letters we learn a lot about what he did and what he thought. For example we know that he liked his Mother-in-law, Dame Elizabeth Rich, but not Katherine's Grandmother, Mistress Croke. He called her "a difficult old lady with a sour tongue". When they met he wrote, "she made me right sullen cheer and I had no joy to stay with her". Thomas married Katherine when she was fifteen and they lived together in London. A year after their marriage, he was very ill and his new bride nursed him and looked after the wool business. When he recovered he once again travelled widely. In the Cotswolds he talked to Whyte of Broadway, a wool dealer, about the wool that would be ready in the summer. He rode round to see the sheep and the quality of their wool before he agreed a price and delivery date with Whyte. When the summer came, he returned along the rough roads to see that Whyte packed and weighed the wool carefully. Thomas had to check that there was no hair, earth or rubbish mixed with the wool as the rules of the Staple Company were very strict about quality. Then packhorses carried the bales of wool south along tracks over the Wiltshire and Hampshire Downs, through Surrey and Kent by the Pilgrims' Way to Maidstone and Rainham. Ships carried the wool from these ports across the sea to Calais. If the ships escaped the pirates and storms at sea, Thomas received the message: "Sir, thanked be the good Lord, I understand that our wool ship be comen in to Calais." Thomas often stayed in Calais. While he was there he lived in a guest house. Sometimes the other guests quarrelled, but Thomas was only in trouble for coming down late to dinner because he took so long writing letters to his wife. In Calais he repacked damaged wool bales and paid the customs duty to the company of the Staple who collected the money for the king. He sold the wool to Peter and Daniel Van de Rade of Bruges in Belgium. The sale took a long time. When Peter and Daniel paid him Thomas kept enough money for the Cotswold wool dealers. Part of the rest he spent in buying presents for his wife. These were fine silks and mink furs which he brought back from special shopping trips to Fairs in Antwerp and Bruges. After seven years of marriage Thomas died, leaving Katherine to look after a family of two sons and three daughters. He was buried near his home, in All Hallows Church, Barking.

Things to do

1 *Complete these sentences using words in the box.*

In the House of Lords the seat covered in red cloth and filled with wool is called the ....

Thomas Betson bought wool in England and sold it in ....

His wool ship escaped the dangers of .... and .... at sea on its journey to Calais.

He bought silks and furs for Katherine at Fairs in .... and.............

> Bruges, pirates, Calais, woolsack, storms, Antwerp

2 *Give a description in your own words of Thomas Betson's work as a wool merchant.*

2   Sheep.

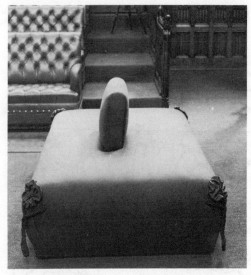

3   The Woolsack.

4   Woolpack Inn, Coggeshall.

25

11 Thomas Paycocke

1   The Fleece Inn, Coggeshall.

2   Dyeing cloth.

3   The Woolpack Inn, Coggeshall.

At first weavers in England made rough cloth. Then, some Belgian weavers came to England and taught the English townsmen how to weave fine cloth from local wool. Most English cloth was made in Essex near Colchester, and in the west of England. In these areas weavers turned wool into cloth. Then dyers dipped pieces of cloth into large vats of hot dye as you can see in the picture. They used bright coloured dyes from plants and roots. Woad made a bright blue dye and this was the most common colour. Madder roots, sold in the Maddermarket at Norwich, made a red dye. Yellow came from saffron found in crocuses. Special saffron yellow crocuses grew round Saffron Walden in Essex. Cloth merchants packed the finished cloth into bundles of twelve rolls. The merchant who owned the cloth stamped his mark onto each bale. Then he sent the cloth to a draper who sold it for him. The mark of an ermine tail showed that a bale of cloth belonged to Thomas Paycocke, a cloth merchant who lived in Coggeshall in Essex. Wool and cloth were so important in the town of Coggeshall that they still call two of the inns "The Woolpack" and "The Fleece". In Thomas's day, the hall that now forms part of the Public Bar at the Woolpack was where the wool sale took place. Thomas's house, called "Paycockes" is still in West Street and has a big garden with a dove house. There are carvings of his mark, the ermine tail, on the front of his house and on the fireplace and ceiling in the hall. The ermine tail looked like a clover leaf. He decorated the woodwork of the house with his initials and those of his first wife, Margaret. His second wife, Anne, whom he called "my good wif" lived longer than he did.

He was a kind employer and cared for his work people and their families. Hum-

26

phrey Stoner, his apprentice was learning about the cloth trade. His fuller, Robert Taylor, treated the cloth with cold water and a special clay called fullers' earth. Thomas Goodday the shearman, smoothed and finished the cloth using long, sharp, flat-ended shears. When Thomas Paycocke died, he left them all some money in his will, although he left the larger part of his wealth to Coggeshall Abbey. On his journeys through the country lanes near Coggeshall, Thomas had often com-

plained about the poor state of the roads. They were muddy in winter and full of holes in summer. So he left money to the town officials to mend part of West Street near his house, and to mend the road between Coggeshall and Blackwater. Many people came to the splendid funeral of Thomas Paycocke for he was the richest cloth merchant of Coggeshall town. In the Church of St Peter Ad Vincula at Coggeshall you can see where Thomas Paycocke's family are buried. There is his brother John, you can see him in the picture, John's wife Joan and his nephew, another Thomas Paycocke.

Things to do

1 Complete these sentences using the words in the box.

.... weavers taught the English townsmen how to weave fine cloth.

.... in Essex and the .... of England were important areas for the cloth trade.

.... finished the cloth.

.... roots made a red dye, and yellow dye came from .... found in crocuses.

The mark of an .... showed that a bale of cloth belonged to Thomas Paycocke.

madder, saffron, west, shearmen, ermine tail, Colchester, Belgian

2 Describe in your own words the work of fullers, shearmen and dyers.

4   John Paycocke.

5   Thomas Paycocke's house at Coggeshall.

12 Guilds

The townspeople who made and sold goods joined together to form a guild. Everybody connected with a trade was a member and had a say in the running of the guild. The employers known as master craftsmen, the workers called journeymen, and the apprentices who were learning the craft, belonged to their own trade guild. In London there were eighty of these separate guilds, one for the goldsmiths, one for the masons who built with stone, one for the fishmongers and many more. In order to become a senior guild member, a journeyman made a "masterpiece". You can see in the picture a member of the guild judging masterpieces which a mason and a carpenter are making. If the masterpiece was good enough, and the craftsman paid a large sum of money to the guild, he could call himself a master craftsman. Then, with the other master craftsmen, he made the rules for their trade at meetings in the guild hall. In York, the rich guild known as "The Company of Merchant Adventurers" had their own guild hall on the banks of the River Foss. They got their name because they "adventured" overseas to trade. The Merchant Adventurers in York traded in cloth with Belgium. The guild fixed the wages for journeymen, limited the number of hours worked each week, and set prices for the goods. They also set standards of good workmanship and punished members who produced poorly

1   The Guild Hall of Merchant Adventurers at York.

finished articles. Each year they chose a leader of the guild called the "master" or "warden", and "searchers" to make certain that members obeyed guild rules. The searchers visited shopkeepers to check that they weighed and measured their goods carefully. They watched for cloth which the shopkeeper folded to hide faults and holes, and they tasted the food which was on sale. To help the searchers find dishonest traders, each merchant had to put his own mark on the goods he made. You can see pictures of merchants' marks on the page opposite. Even though the guilds made these checks, customers sometimes bought faulty or unfinished goods. If they complained to the guild, the guild forced the member to mend or complete his work. If it was a very bad mistake

the warden expelled the cheating craftsman from the guild. This happened to Roger Aldrith of Leicester after he had three times sold poor quality scarlet cloth.

Most craftsmen however, produced excellent work as you can see in the picture of Canterbury Cathedral. This was the work of Master Mason-Architects William of Sens and William the Englishman. As members of the guild, the craftsmen had many benefits. The guilds did not allow non members to trade in the town and they cared for the unemployed, sick, and families of those who died. In many towns they had sufficient money to build houses, called almshouses, for these people. The rich Taylors' Guild built Merchant Taylors School in London.

2 Mark of Thomas Pownder.

3 Mark of John Lambard.

4 Mark of Walter Hichman.

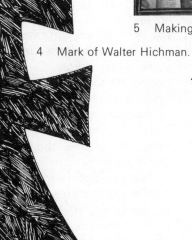

5 Making a masterpiece.

6 Canterbury Cathedral.

Things to do

1 *Complete these sentences using the words in the box.*

Townspeople who made and sold goods joined together to form a ....

Employers in a guild were called ....

The .... were learning a trade.

.... made sure that members obeyed guild rules.

.... was the work of William of Sens and William the Englishman.

> master craftsmen, searchers,
> Canterbury Cathedral,
> guild, apprentices

2 *How did guilds punish cheating workmen?*

3 *Describe how guilds looked after members when they were old or sick.*

4 *What work did the Merchant Adventurers do, and where in York did they have their guild hall?*

13 Craftsmen

1 Apprentice fishmonger.

The youngest members of a guild were called apprentices. When a boy was about twelve years old his father agreed to pay a master craftsman to teach his boy a trade. The master was paid to teach the apprentice his job and to look after him as well. He clothed and fed his pupil and punished him if he gambled or wasted time with his friends. The agreement between father and master craftsman was called an indenture. Each of them kept a copy. The two copies were cut at the edges to form a shape which fitted together like two jig-saw pieces. This proved that they were not forgeries. From the day this agreement was signed and for the following seven years, the boy lived with the master craftsman as one of the family. He was not paid and, at first, just ran errands and watched the master at work. Gradually he was given more and more difficult jobs to do. For example, a fishmonger's apprentice learnt how to catch eels and salmon and how to collect mussels. He learnt how to keep fish fresh by storing them in salt. You can see a picture of the apprentice showing two fish to customers in the fish shop.

A mason's apprentice learnt how to split stones into the correct size by hammering thin iron wedges into them. He watched the master shape the stones with chisels and a mallet. In the picture on the next page you can see the tools used in building. The workmen are using a simple crane to lift up a bucket of bricks, a spirit level for checking that the bricks are laid flat, and a plumb line to check that the wall is straight. On some medieval churches the masons carved faces on the stone water spouts. These are called gargoyles. The rainwater from the roof ran along gutters and out through the mouths of the gargoyles to fall onto the ground below. The masons often made the faces look like people they disliked, or like devils or fantastic monsters.

At the end of seven years the apprentice took a test set by the guild, and if he passed he became a journeyman. He was now paid a daily wage for his work. As a journeyman he had to take another test set by the guild wardens and produce an example of his work called a masterpiece. If the officers of his guild thought his work was good enough, and if he could afford to pay a large subscription to the guild he could set up a shop and work on his own. He was now a master craftsman and ready to train apprentices himself.

Things to do

1   *Complete these sentences using the words in the box.*

    The .... were the youngest members of a guild.

    Father and master craftsman made an agreement called an ....

    An apprenticeship lasted for .... years.

    Carved stone water spouts are called ....

    A .... was paid a daily wage.

> seven, apprentices, gargoyles, indenture, journeyman

2   *Make up an account in your own words of a day's work in the life of an apprentice fishmonger.*

2   Apprentice masons.

3   *Why did masons put carved stone water spouts on churches?*

4   *Draw or trace the gargoyles on this page.*

3   Gargoyles.

14 Mystery Plays

1 The Guild of Smiths present the Trial of Christ.

In early June, on the day of the Festival of Corpus Christi, all the townspeople had a holiday. Villagers from the surrounding area joined the townsmen in a procession through the streets. They enjoyed the procession, took part in the dancing and singing, but they liked most of all the plays acted in the open air on wooden wagons called pageants. The pageant was very tall and was divided into two compartments. The lower floor had curtains all round it and was used as a dressing room for the actors. The upper platform was the stage, where the actors gave their play and kept all their scenery. Horses dragged the pageants to special places called pageant stations, in the open spaces and streets of the town. At these stations, a large crowd of noisy local people watched the plays, frequently adding their shouts to the words of the actors. As religion was most important to all medieval townsmen, and formed a very large part of their lives, the plays showed stories from the Bible. They told of the Creation, the Birth, Crucifixion and Return to Life of Jesus, and the Life of the Virgin Mary. Each play ended with the story of the Last Judgement.

Actors made the people in the Bible stories appear very like people known to the audience. Herod and Pilate were a pair of swaggering bullies. Noah's wife was a bossy and badtempered woman. The characters always wore the same clothes so that the audience recognised them easily. Herod wore a Saracen's outfit, as you see in the picture. Angels wore white robes and blonde wigs, while demons had ugly masks and made horrible noises. Judas had red hair, and the Devil also had red hair as well as horns and a tail. Anyone sent to Hell dropped through a trap door into the dressing room. The actors underneath the stage rattled stones in a barrel to make the sound of an earthquake for the Crucifixion, and lit candles to give the bright light which came when Jesus appeared on Earth again. The actors in the plays, who played both men's and women's parts, were members of a guild. The word used for craft guilds was "misteries", and so townsmen called their guild plays "mystery plays". Each guild produced a play connected with its trade. The Goldsmiths acted the story of the Three Wise Men and their precious gifts. The wool merchants chose the Shepherds at Bethlehem, and the Shipbuilders told the story of the building of Noah's Ark. The favourite of the Fishmongers was of course the Adventures of Jonah and the Whale. The guilds competed to give the most entertaining play. The craft guild which built the best scenery and had the most colourful costumes was the best guild for the following year. So the members paid "pageant silver" to buy the costumes and made every effort to act their parts well. A guild fined poor actors, but paid "transfer fees" to buy good actors from a rival craft guild.

2 Herod.

Things to do

1 *Complete these sentences using the words in the box.*
Townspeople had a .... on the Festival of Corpus Christi.
They watched plays performed on wooden wagons called ....
.... dragged the pageants to pageant stations in the town streets.
The plays showed stories from the ....

3 A scene from a York Mystery Play.
All the actors belonged to a ....
Townsmen called the plays ....
....

horses, pageants, holiday, Bible, mystery plays, guild

2 *Imagine you are a medieval townsman and describe some of the mystery plays you watched on the Festival of Corpus Christi.*
3 *Explain how you would recognise the actors playing Herod, Judas and the Devil.*

33

15 Plays at York and Chester

1 Scene from 1969 cycle of plays at York.

A group of mystery plays, performed one after another, is called a "cycle" of plays. In some towns the cycle lasted for three days, but in most towns guilds put on all their plays in one day by starting soon after sunrise. Each guild gave a different play on its own pageant wagon. Even the sleepy early morning audience understood the simple words used. For example, Noah invited his wife into the Ark with:

"Welcome, wife, into this boat". Noah's wife, always a comic character, replied: "Have thou this for thy note", and boxed Noah on the ears!

Not all the plays in the Chester Cycle contained this type of slap-stick comedy. We know from the copies of the words which are still in existence, that many of them told serious Bible stories. The Drapers acted the Creation of the World and the Slaters and Thatchers the Birth of

Our Lord. The cycle lasted in Chester for three days, and the guilds performed twenty-five separate plays. A monk called Ralph Higden wrote all the plays. He had to go three times to Rome to get the Pope's permission to write his plays in English instead of Church Latin. He used some special tricks in the performances. He sent sinners down to Hell through a trap door in the pageant floor and gave Moses a walking stick which suddenly grew flowers as if by magic! The Chester Cycle is still performed every five years and the York Plays more often, once every three years. You can see pictures of scenes from plays acted in York in 1969. There, they showed all the forty-eight plays in one day. On the evening before, a man on horseback rode through the streets of York telling people to come to the plays the next day. He also warned them to leave their weapons at home and to watch without "assault, affray or other disturbance". At 4.30 in the morning the pageant wagons arrived at the first station near Micklegate and the guild members gave their first performance of the day. In York, men dragged the wagons through the streets after each performance. The Bakers' Guild were rich enough to pay six labourers to do this work rather than push their cart themselves. The Butchers performed the Crucifixion, and the Bakers the Last Supper. In other plays, guildsmen playing the parts of devils wore coats decorated with hair and feathers. They made a large painted dragon's head for

34

2   Micklegate Bar, York.

the mouth of Hell as you see in the picture. They made model animals for their plays from canvas and wood. Important buildings such as Herod's Palace and the Temple in Jerusalem were only the size of sentry boxes in order to fit onto the small stage. All the performances finished at nine o'clock in the evening.

3   The mouth of hell.

King Richard II was a special guest at the plays in 1397. The records show that he watched from a box near the first pageant station. He cost the townspeople of York a lot of money for they had to provide new uniforms of red and white for his servants, food and drink for his courtiers, as well as pay extra people to push the wagons away quickly as each play finished.

Things to do

1   *Complete these sentences using the words in the box.*
The Chester Cycle of plays lasted for .... days.
In York they showed all the forty-eight plays in .... day.
A monk called .... wrote the plays at Chester.

King .... watched the York Plays in 1397.

three,   Ralph Higden,   Richard II, one

2   *Draw and label the diagram of a pageant wagon.*

4   Diagram of a pageant wagon.

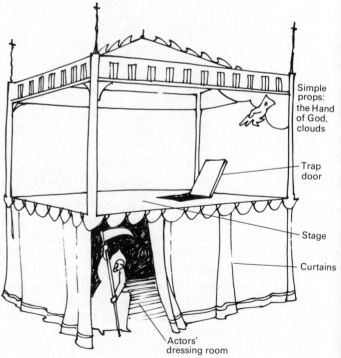

Simple props: the Hand of God, clouds

Trap door

Stage

Curtains

Actors' dressing room

16 Fairs and Markets

1   Fish and vegetable market.

Country folk brought fresh food from their villages to sell in the town market. They set up stalls in an open space as you can see in this picture of a fish and vegetable market. York had a market selling corn, food and drink on Tuesday, Thursday and Saturday of each week. Because the market was in the town, villagers bringing food to sell, had to follow the rules set by the townspeople. Firstly, they had to pay a tax on all the goods they brought through the town gates. Secondly, they had to allow guild searchers to check the food on their stalls and make sure it was of good quality. Bernard Horner sold meat in York market. When his customers complained, officials found that two searchers had not inspected his bad meat, so they punished them as well as Bernard. If the townspeople wanted goods that they could not buy in their own town, they travelled to a special market called a fair.

Only the large towns held fairs. They lasted for three to seven days and took place once a year. Fairs were too large to hold in the crowded town streets and so they were held on a large, open space outside the walls, called the Fairground.

Each trade gathered in its own area of the Fairground. For example, all wine-sellers set up stalls together and all candle-makers were next to one another, just as they were in their shops in the town streets. Local traders and farmers sold their goods at the fair, but most of the merchants came from other parts of England or from foreign countries. They sold silks from Baghdad in Iraq, spices from Egypt, and armour, satin and silver ornaments from Germany. Traders from Norway and Sweden sold fur coats and also hawks, which the townsmen used for catching pigeons and duck. Townspeople paid for the goods they bought with silver pennies. Cheaper articles cost a half penny, which was a penny cut in half, and for some things, quarter pennies called farthings were enough. In the picture two merchants are counting their money at the end of a fair. The one on the right is using a counting frame, called an abacus, while the merchant on the left is writing down the same figures as we use today.

Because of the large crowds at the fair, townspeople always had to be on guard against pickpockets and tricksters. One trader talked a bishop into buying "a never-before-seen animal from the Holy Land", which was in fact a stuffed

2 Silver penny of Henry II, a half penny and a farthing.

3 The bishop blesses a fair.

4 Merchants counting money.

mouse! There was a special law court, called the Court of Pie Powder or Dusty Feet, which listened only to disputes and quarrels from the fair. It settled these quarrels quickly before strangers left the fair. When the court decided to punish a trader, it fined him or left him for two or three hours in the stocks. Henry I's court jester called Rahere, started St Bartholomew's Fair at Smithfield in London. Rahere was a clever business man and got a licence from the King to run his three day Fair. It started as a cloth fair, and Cloth Fair is still the name of a street near Smithfield. Now, Smithfield is London's great Meat Market.

Things to do

1 *Complete these sentences using the words in the box.*
   Villagers paid a .... on goods they brought to market.
   Guild .... checked the food to make sure it was of good ....
   Large towns held fairs on the ....
   The Court of .... settled quarrels at the fair.

> quality, tax, Fairground,
> searchers, Pie Powder

17 Sickness and Doctors

1   Bleeding a patient.

Many people died from illness in medieval times because doctors did not have much idea how to cure sickness. The townspeople had to face simple illnesses as well as leprosy and plagues that we do not meet today. They did not know the real cause of their illnesses or why they spread through the towns so fast. We know that smelly overcrowded towns, rats, and dirty drinking water all helped disease to spread quickly. The priests thought that God sent sickness to punish the townsmen, and so they told people to pray and wait till they became well again. Those who wanted to get better more quickly went to an alchemist or a doctor. The alchemist was a man who looked both for a way to turn ordinary metals into gold and for a medicine to cure all illnesses. Some of the medicine he handed out was useful, for example a Portuguese alchemist found that brandy helped sick people to feel better. The doctor was superstitious, and he believed that magic could help his patients. He thought that there were lucky and unlucky days for making people better, so he always asked his patient for the date of his birth before deciding how he should cure the illness. The usual treatment was to bleed some of the blood from the patient as you see in the picture. This made the patient more ill, but at least was not so strange as the cure for a broken head. For in this the doctor brushed the injured head with a fox's foot which would hardly heal the bones! Priests did not allow doctors to study dead bodies and find out how they worked. Although they knew very little about science, doctors learned by experience the right things to do for each patient. In the picture you can see a doctor wondering what to do about his patient with a spotty face. He is holding another patient over a bowl of burning herbs to make his headache better. Patients paid for their treatment, and it cost them a lot of money. Doctors usually asked for half of their money before starting the treatment, and waited to collect the rest when the patient got better. For many simple illnesses, the doctor gave his patient some medicine. An apothecary, called a chemist today, mixed medicines from strange powders, insects and herbs, and sold the medicine and ointments he made to anyone who

3 Patients with headache and spots.

2 Advertisement for Doctor John Case.

asked for his help. He used spiders in butter, ants' eggs, and even magpies' beaks, for apothecaries said that a magpie's beak hung round the neck cured a sore throat, and that a necklace of spiders cured 'flu. They also used herbs for ointments, mixed with strange things like powdered earthworms and crushed beetles. In many towns rogues and tricksters pretended to be doctors, telling all kinds of lies about their cures as you can see in the advertisement on this page. They offered to cure deafness, make blind people see and pretended to have wonderful new and expensive medicines. Unfortunately when the townsmen found out that these were useless they no longer believed in the treatments of doctors who really were trying to make them well again.

Things to do

1   *Complete these sentences using the words in the box.*
    Many townspeople died from........ illnesses which doctors could not cure.
    Overcrowded towns ...., and dirty drinking .... helped disease to spread quickly.
    The .... searched for a medicine to cure all illnesses.
    An .... is called a chemist today.

> rats, alchemist, simple, water, apothecary

2   *How would your doctor today treat a patient with a broken or fractured head?*

39

18 Surgeons and Hospitals

1   A barber-surgeon pulling out a tooth.

Visitors to a medieval town were certain to see the sign of a red and white striped pole outside a shop. This pole was supposed to be a bandaged, bleeding arm, and it showed that a surgeon who also cut hair worked inside. In those days the barber-surgeon stopped wounds from bleeding, pulled out teeth, and mended broken arms and legs. He taught his apprentices how to cut hair carefully, stitch big wounds, and make plaster moulds to mend broken legs.

All this treatment was very painful. The surgeon knew, however, that some plant juices made the pain less. So he used the juice from poppy flowers which contains a little morphine, a drug still used in hospitals today. There were medieval hospitals where they looked after the sick in the same way as they do now. In fact some of our hospitals started in the Middle Ages. St Bartholomew's Hospital is still in the same place in London as the first building

paid for by King Henry I's court jester, Rahere. He chose a good place for his Hospital, for the tournaments fought on the Smoothfield, or Smithfield in front of the building gave him many patients. Rahere is buried in the Hospital Chapel and it is said that his ghost still walks there! Some of the hospitals only took patients suffering from one kind of disease. For example the hospitals for lepers, built outside the town walls, only looked after lepers. There was no treatment for the lepers in these hospitals, but they stayed away from the townspeople to stop the disease spreading. When they had to go into the town to beg for food and money, lepers carried rattles and wooden clappers to warn people to keep away from them. Mad or insane people stayed at the Hospital of St Mary of Bethlehem in London, called Bedlam. They were not treated kindly, for the records of 1398 show that nurses used iron chains, locks and stocks to keep the patients from escaping or harming themselves. Townspeople thought that mad people were like animals and they went to laugh at the poor lunatics in their cells, and the hospital was a special tourist attraction in London. Even though there was no treatment, some lunatics did get better. Then they begged in the streets of London for food and clothing to give the lunatics still inside. They wore brass badges to show who they were, and they blew oxhorn trumpets to attract attention. Most of the hospital patients died because they caught a

40

2   A barber-surgeon and his patients.

dangerous disease either from the other patients in hospital, or from dirty wards and bandages. It was a long, long time before hospitals cured more patients than they buried.

4   Rahere's tomb, St Bartholomew's Hospital Chapel.

3   Rahere.

Things to do

1   *Complete these sentences using the words in the box.*
A striped pole hung outside a
.... shop.
Lepers lived in hospitals outside the
....
.... built St Bartholomew's Hospital.

> towns, Rahere, barber-surgeon's

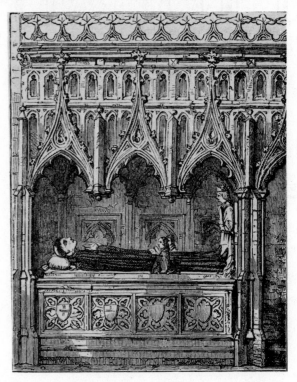

2   *Make a list of the work of a barber-surgeon.*
3   *What sort of work does a surgeon do in a modern hospital?*

19 Doctor Andrew Borde

Doctor Boorde.

1 Doctor Andrew Borde.

Many medieval doctors were superstitious men who could not cure their patients or give good advice to those who asked for help. A few, however, who had listened to clever doctors teaching in Europe, and who had a lot of "common sense" were good. One such good man, Doctor Andrew Borde, not only tried to cure sickness but thought out new ways to stop people becoming ill. His ideas on how to live a healthy life still work today. When he left school, Andrew became a monk, but after twenty years decided to change his job and learn how to be a doctor. He listened to wise doctors in France and Sweden, and visited Spain, Portugal, Italy and the Holy Land. After this long journey round Europe and the Middle East, he treated his first patients in London, before settling down to live in Winchester, Hampshire. Here he wrote a very interesting book called "A Dietary of Health". It told people how to stay healthy and described some simple cures for patients to try themselves. In the book he described the causes of illnesses and the cures in a simple way which the townspeople understood easily. The Doctor had no time for the strange words, secret ways and magic spells of his fellow doctors and apothecaries. So he told people how to live a healthy life. He knew there were many diseases in towns, so he wanted people to live in the countryside. He said they should build houses close to fresh drinking water, and near woodland where they could find firewood to keep their houses warm. He told them to grow apple trees for fresh fruit, keep deer and rabbits for fresh meat, and fill the fishponds with fish. They should not build houses near stagnant water, marshes or misty land, as good clean air kept people well. Doctor Borde thought that exercise made people healthy and he told patients to take an early morning walk of a thousand paces, then play tennis or bowls. He also thought that archery was a good sport for keeping people healthy. He did not like his patients wearing damp clothes, sitting on cold stones or staying out, without a hat, in cold weather. He liked them to wear jackets lined with sheepskin for the winter and keep out of the hot sun in summer. He warned people not to over-eat, and said that two meals a day were enough for his patients. Most important of all, he said that happy people were healthy people, and that worries, especially about money, made people sick and unhappy. If, after all this good advice, a patient fell ill, Doctor Borde told the household to choose good nurses to care for the sick man, and keep noisy visitors out of the sick room. In the picture you can see a doctor taking his patient's pulse to find how fast his heart was beating. Doctor Borde agreed with this careful, scientific method of finding out why a patient was sick.

Things to do

1 *Complete these sentences using the words in the box.*
Andrew Borde listened to wise doctors in .... and the Middle East.
He wrote a book called ....
....
There were many diseases in ...., so he wanted people to live in the ....

2 Picture from Doctor Borde's book.

Doctor Borde said .... people were healthy people.

towns, happy, Europe,
A Dietary of Health, countryside

2 *Make a list of Doctor Borde's ideas on how to live a healthy life.*
3 *Draw a picture of the house and garden described in this chapter.*

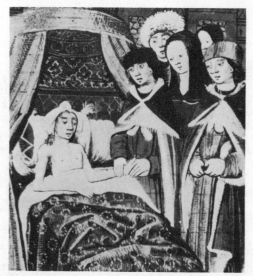

3 A doctor taking his patient's pulse.

4 Playing bowls.

20 London

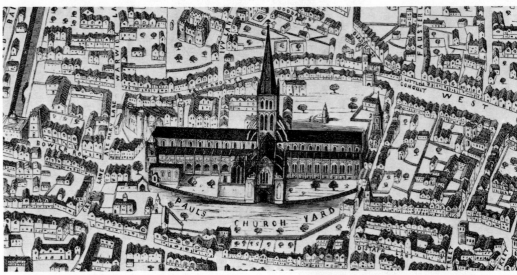

1   Old St Paul's Cathedral.

2   The Tower of London.

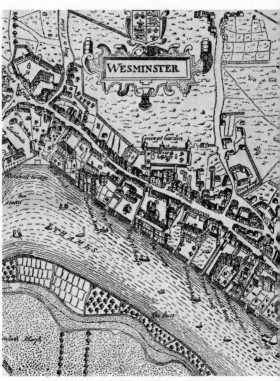

3   Houses on the Strand.

London was England's largest city. It was a port, a shopping centre and many of the richest guild merchants in the land lived there. Even so, it was much, much smaller than it is today. There were fields close to the centre, and in the forests beyond, Londoners hunted stags and boars (wild pigs). A wall surrounded the City itself, running round the area between the Tower of London in the East and Ludgate in the West. This is now the part of London where you find the banks, insurance and office buildings.

In modern times the City has spread far outside the old walls, and to the separate City of Westminster further down the River Thames. In medieval times most Londoners travelled by boat down the Thames from Westminster to the City. They passed the splendid houses of rich

44

merchants on the Strand, which was a main road even in those days. These houses had gardens running down to the river and landing stages for the merchants' barges. Nearer the City there were crowds of boats on the River. Some brought farm produce to the markets, and stately barges carried noblemen and ladies to their houses on the Strand. By far the largest number were the small boats called wherries in which watermen ferried people and goods across the River. The only other way to cross the River into the City of London from the south was over London Bridge. The Bridge, crowded with houses and shops, was one of the wonders of the times, and many people came to London specially to see it. The best view of the gleaming white Tower of London was also from the River. It was built by William the Conqueror and still stands today as you can see in the photo taken from the Thames. In the Middle Ages the Tower belonged to the King and he kept a Royal Mint there to make silver pennies. Henry II's pet elephant stayed in the Tower, too, and Henry III kept an elephant and a lion there. You can find out more about the Tower of London in the book *Knights and Castles* in this series. In the centre of the City stood the huge building of Old St Paul's Cathedral. It towered above the narrow streets and gold flashed from the large cross at the top of the spire. A stone from Christ's burial place in the Holy Land was put inside the cross to keep it safe in stormy weather.

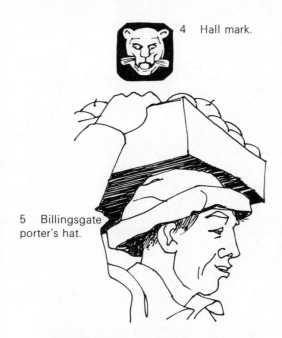

4   Hall mark.

5   Billingsgate porter's hat.

6   Billingsgate porter.

In contrast to the peace and quiet of the Cathedral the street markets were very noisy indeed. You can still see the Fish Market at Billingsgate and the porters there carry the loads of fish on their heads balanced on large hats made of cork and leather, just as they did in medieval times. Visitors bought goods and food from the shops of the guild craftsmen. The most famous groups of shops and houses were those of the Goldsmiths in Foster Row. From 1300 all gold and silver plate and jewellery made in London and sold in their shops had to have the London Goldsmiths' mark of a leopard's head. Today, this "hall mark" of the London Goldsmiths is still a guarantee of good workmanship.

Things to do

1   *Complete these sentences using the words in the box.*

    .... was England's largest city.
    Rich merchants lived in splendid houses on the ....
    Small boats called .... ferried people across the River.
    .... built the Tower of London.

Strand, William the Conqueror, London, wherries

2   *Describe the houses and buildings you could see from the River Thames in medieval times.*

Newcastle

Durham

Preston

Bolton

Liverpool

Conway

Chester

York

Nottingham

Leicester

King's Lynn

Norwich

Coventry

Blythburgh

Banbury

Cambridge

Lavenham

Saffron
Walden

Colchester

Coggeshall

Northleach

Cotswolds

Bath

LONDON

Rochester

Canterbury

Maidstone

Sandwich

Barnstaple

Winchester

Dover

Bideford

Hythe

Romney

Hastings

*Isles of
Scilly*

1   Towns mentioned in this book.

2 A Lord Mayor of London.
   What was the name of this Lord Mayor
   of London?

3 Stonegate in York.
   Look at this photo of Stonegate in
   York today. How can you tell from the
   street and the houses that this was
   once a medieval street?

5 John Lyndewode.
   How do we know from this picture of
   John Lyndewode that he was a wool
   merchant? Can you find and copy
   John's merchant's mark?

4 Walled garden.
   You can see townsfolk in a walled
   garden inside the town. Why did these
   gardens have to be small?

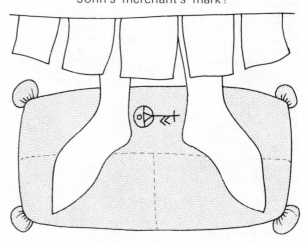

Index